B-52

Osprey Colour Series

B-52

Ageing BUFFs
Youthful Crews

René J Francillon and Peter B Lewis

Published in 1988 by Osprey Publishing Limited
27A Floral Street, London WC2E 9DP
Member company of the George Philip Group

British Library Cataloguing in Publication Data

Françillon, René J. (René Jacquet), *1937–*
  B-52; ageing BUFFs, youthful crews.
  1. Boeing B-52 aeroplanes
  I. Title   II. Lewis, Peter B.
  623.74′63
ISBN 0–85045–863–3

Editor Dennis Baldry
Additional photography by Jim Dunn, Bud Joyce, Karl Kornchuk,
Tony Muniz, Carl E Porter, Brian C Rogers and the United States
Air Force
Designed by Paul Butters
Printed in Hong Kong

Front cover The majestic sight of a Boeing
B-52G Stratofortress overflying Castle AFB in
California. As can be seen, this example (57-
6495) has been fitted with wing root extensions.
These indicate that the aircraft is capable of
carrying ALCMs (Air-Launched Cruise Missiles).
Part of the SALT 2 accords, this modification
was introduced to enable the Soviet Union to
verify the number of cruise-capable B-52s by
using satellite photography

Title pages Thundering and billowing smoke, a
B-52G-100-BW (58-0195) of the 93rd
Bombardment Wing lifts off at Castle AFB on 23
May 1983

Right Seated on a downward ejecting seat on
the right-hand side of the lower deck, the
navigator shares duties and responsibilities with
the radar navigator who sits on his left. The two
screens at eye-level are an Electro-optical
Viewing System (EVS) monitor and a radar
indicator. Control panels for the AGM-69A Short-
Range Attack Missiles (SRAMs) are just above
the navigator's left hand

Back cover The 44-foot ribbon-type drag chute
can be deployed at 135 knots IAS. Deployment
at higher speeds may result in failure of the
chute or shear pin. The risers of the main chute
are attached to the aircraft through a terminal
held by the jettison mechanism

In 1960, five years after the B-52 had entered service with the 93rd Bombardment Wing at Castle AFB, California, a Soviet surface-to-air missile brought down the high-flying U-2 of Francis Gary Powers. It was enough for pundits the world over to announce the end of the manned bomber era. Even within Strategic Air Command, many were those who saw little future for the B-52. In their opinion, switching from high altitude operations to low-level penetration and making increased use of stand-off weapons were at best short-term palliatives. Indeed, from a peak strength of 32 Bombardment Wings and six Strategic Aerospace Wings in 1963 (with 636 B-52s and 593 Hound Dog missiles), the force was allowed to dwindle slowly and the first Stratofortress operational model, the B/RB-52B, began to be phased out in 1965 after a typical 10-year operational life.

Although the Southeast Asia War provided a new lease of life for the B-52 when *Arc Light* operations were initiated in June 1965, opponents of the manned bomber concept remained smug in their belief that the Big Ugly Fat Fellow could only be used as a 'flying bomb truck' against undefended targets. However, these critics were confounded by the success achieved by B-52s during *Linebacker II*, when in spite of the heaviest concentration of guns and missiles ever seen, losses were kept to an acceptable level (15 B-52s were lost in the course of 729 sorties against targets in Hanoi and Haiphong; 28 aircrew members were killed or missing in action and 33 were taken POWs).

A third of a century after 52-7811 was delivered to Castle AFB, the flying Methusalah again and again proves doomsayers wrong. The B-52 will not live 969 years like the biblical patriach but it will undoubtedly have the longest operational career of any military aircraft. Some B-52s may still be wearing the SAC shield on 15 April 2002, when it will be time to celebrate the 50th anniversary of the XB-52's first flight. At that time, the first generation of intercontinental ballistic missiles will already have been retired for 37 years!

We wish to express our sincere appreciation to the United States Air Force and especially to the staff of the Media and Civil Relations Division, Office of Public Affairs, Headquarters Strategic Air Command, for the support they provided during the preparation of this photographic tribute to the B-52. Special thanks go to the late Major Deverl H Johnson, the Airfield Manager at Castle AFB, who proved a source of inspiration, and to two instructor KC-135 boom operators, MSgt Samuel Hunt of the 924th AREFS and TSgt Donald L Houchin of the 93rd AREFS, who patiently let us 'elbow them' while photographing refuelling activities on 23 May 1984 and 17 November 1987. Last but not least, we most sincerely thank 1Lt Stephanie Johnson, 320th BMW/PA, and our 93rd BMW/PA friends—1Lt Brian Settler, SRA Scott Carter, and A1C Susan Rau—for all their help during our visits to Mather AFB and Castle AFB.

René J Françillon & Peter B Lewis
Vallejo, California, February 1988

Like the local farmers and ranchers, cattle have become oblivious to the coming and going of noisy aircraft and keep on grazing while a B-52G-85-BW lands at Castle AFB. The snow-covered Sierra Nevada can be seen in the background on this unusually clear spring day in 1979

Contents

BUFFs in the buff

The third B-52A (52-0003) was modified as the carrier for the X-15 high-speed/high altitude research aircraft and, fitted with a special pylon under the starboard wing root, was redesignated NB-52A. It is seen here at Edwards AFB, California, in May 1967. The blue and white badge beneath the cockpit is that of the Air Force Systems Command

Right Serial 56-0632, the second B-52E built in Seattle, was modified as a control-configured research vehicle and was assigned to the Air Force Flight Dynamics Laboratory. After completion of trials the aircraft was sent to the Military Aircraft Storage & Disposition Center (MASDC) at Davis-Monthan AFB, Arizona, where it was photographed on 15 May 1975

Left A total of 100 B-52Es were accepted by the Air Force between October 1957 and July 1958. The last operational B-52Es were phased out by the 22nd and 96th Bombardment Wings in 1970. 57-0119, a B-52E-55-BW, was modified as a test bed for the General Electric TF39 turbofans which were to power Lockheed C-5As. For that purpose, an XTF39 replaced the two J57-P-29WAs in the No 3 nacelle of this NB-52E

Above The first powered test of a North American GAM-77 Hound Dog stand-off missile was made in April 1959, the missile being launched over the Gulf Test Range from a modified B-52D. Redesignated AGM-28 in 1962, the Hound Dog was first carried operationally by B-52Fs fitted with an underwing pylon on each side of the fuselage. An AGM-28A can be seen beneath the left wing of this B-52F-100-BO of the 320th Bombardment Wing photographed at Mather AFB, California, on 28 October 1967

Top right After serving with the 320th Bombardment Wing at Mather AFB and flying 50 *Arc Light* missions over South Vietnam, this B-52F-195-BO (57-0044) ended its flying career with the 93rd Bombardment Wing at Castle AFB. Photographed in storage at Davis-Monthan AFB, this aircraft has the MASDC inventory number BC 046 painted forward of the main entrance door

Right The 93rd Bombardment Wing received its first RB-52B (52-8711) on 29 June 1955. Remaining based at Castle AFB, in California's San Joaquin Valley, the 93rd has since been SAC's primary B-52 aircrew training organization. In that capacity, it has been equipped at various times with B-52Bs, B-52Es, B-52Fs (including 57-0070 seen here in storage at MASDC), B-52Gs (first in 1966–67 and continuously since 1974), and B-52Hs

Top left When photographed at Castle AFB on 8 June 1971, this B-52F-70-BW (57-0159) was already at the end of its life. A little more than two months later, on 16 August, it was transferred to MASDC. The 93rd Bombardment Wing received its first B-52Fs in 1958 to train crews for the operational B-52F wings, the 7th Bombardment Wing at Carswell AFB and the 4134th, 4228th and 4238th Strategic Wings respectively at Mather AFB, Columbus AFB, and Barksdale AFB

Left Back from U-Tapao RTNAF, Thailand, where it had been temporarily attached to the 4528th Strategic Wing for *Arc Light* operations, this B-52F-70-BW of the 320th Bombardment Wing had flown 30 operational missions prior to returning to Mather AFB where it was

photographed at the start of California's rainy season on 28 October 1967. After demonstrating in 1964 the B-52's capability to deliver conventional bombs during tests at Eglin AFB, Florida, the 320th BMW joined the 7th BMW in flying the first *Arc Light* mission on 18 June 1965

Above *Thunder Express*, a B-52F-70-BW of the 320th Bombardment Wing flew a total of 68 bombing missions in South Vietnam and along the Ho Chi Minh Trail. Although critics of the war considered *Arc Light* to be ineffective, interrogations of captured VC and NVA personnel demonstrated that Communist insurgents greatly feared high-flying B-52s, as the first sign of an attack were bomb explosions

15

Right 57-6474, one of the first B-52Gs assigned for crew training to the 93rd Bombardment Wing, was photographed at Castle AFB on 21 May 1966. The shorter vertical tail surface and smaller external tanks were the primary recognition features distinguishing the Gs from earlier Stratofortress models. By the time the 93rd got its first B-52Gs, this version had already been in Air Force service for seven years

Below When in July 1968 the 5th Bombardment Wing was transferred from Travis AFB, California, to Minot AFB, North Dakota, to take-over the B-52Hs and facilities of the 450th Bombardment Wing which was being inactivated, its B-52Gs remained in California to replace the war-weary B-52Fs of the 320th Bombardment Wing. 59-2595, a B-52G-120-BW, is seen here at Mather AFB ten months after its transfer to the 320th

Overleaf California has had more B-52 bases than any other state. Three were and two still are operational bases: Beale AFB (4126th Strategic Wing from 1960 until 1963, 456th Strategic Aerospace Wing between 1963 and 1972, and 456th BMW between 1972 and 1975), Castle AFB (93rd BMW since 1955), March AFB (22nd BMW from 1963 until 1982), Mather AFB (4134th Strategic Wing between 1958 and 1963 and 320th BMW since 1963), and Travis AFB (5th BMW between 1959 and 1968). In addition, B-52s have been flying off and on from the Air Force Flight Center at Edwards AFB since the 1950s. The Hound Dog-carrying B-52G seen landing at another California base, McClellan AFB, in June 1965 belonged to the 456th Strategic Aerospace Wing

Right Located 20 miles south of Marquette in Michigan, just south of the Canadian border, K I Sawyer AFB has been a B-52H base since 1961 when the 4042nd Strategic Wing received its aircraft. On 1 February 1963, the 4042nd SW, which like other wings with four digits in the numerical portion of their designation was a temporary SAC-controlled organization, was replaced by the 410th Bombardment Wing, a permanent Air Force-controlled organization. This B-52H-145-BW of the 644th Bombardment Squadron, 410th BMW, was photographed at K I Sawyer AFB on 11 July 1968

Left When on 1 February 1963, the 319th Bombardment Wing was organized, it took over the aircraft and facilities of the inactivated 4133rd Strategic Wing at Grand Forks AFB, North Dakota. Its 46th Bombardment Squadron then flew B-52Hs (including this B-52H-145-BW on the ramp at Grand Forks AFB on 15 July 1968) until converting to Rockwell B-1Bs in 1987. The Hound Dog missile, which was retained in the inventory until 1976, had a top speed of Mach 2.1 and a maximum range of 700 miles. It carried a 1 Mt thermonuclear warhead

Taking over facilities and aircraft from the
4239th Strategic Wing, the 449th Bombardment
Wing flew B-52Hs from February 1963 until
September 1977 when it was inactivated. During
this 14-year period it remained based at
Kincheloe AFB, Michigan, where this B-52H-155-
BW was photographed on 7 July 1968

After leaving its B-52Gs in California when it
was transferred to North Dakota in July 1968,
the 450th Bombardment Wing inherited B-52Hs
from the inactivated 450th Bombardment Wing.
This photograph was taken on 15 July 1968,
exactly ten days before the transfer from the
450th to the 5th took place; the shield emblem
beneath the cockpit is that of the 450th BMW.
Twenty years later, the 5th BMW still flies B-
52Hs from Minot AFB

Heads or tails

Left Taken from atop a maintenance stand, this overhead view provides details of the nose of a B-52G. The bump in front of the windshield houses the antenna for the AN/ALT-28 noise jammer

Right Seen from the boom operator station of a KC-135R, the nose of this B-52G again shows the fairing over the AN/ALT-28 antenna as well as the two side fairings over the forward antennas of the AN/ALQ-117 deception jammer. The white dot on the tip of the upward-hinging radome is more mundane: a spot of icing accumulated during the climb to 30,000 ft through, on this occasion, far from sunny California skies

Above Breaking through the typical winter fog of the Sacramento Valley, early morning sun rays bring a glow to the dull camouflage now standard for B-52Gs and B-52Hs. The intake just forward of the AN/ALQ-117 fairing on the right side is an air cooling inlet for some of the electronic equipment

Top right Nose details of 59-2594, a B-52G-129-BW, photographed at Tyndall AFB, Florida, on 23 September 1978. The emblem, much smaller than those painted earlier when B-52s were not camouflaged, is that of the 2nd Bombardment Wing. The twin steerable EVS turrets beneath the nose have been rotated 180° to keep dust and abrasive materials from damaging the sensitive electro-optical equipment

Right The centre portion of the pilots' instrument panel is filled with eight columns of engine dials. The upper row is occupied by engine pressure ratio gauges, the second row by engine tachometers, the third row by exhaust gas temperature gauges, and the fourth row by fuel flowmeters. Next to these sets of dials are the EVS monitors, one for the aircraft commander and one for the copilot, and, further outboard, attitude-director indicators and horizontal situation indicators. The aisle stand is dominated by the throttles and, to the left, the stabilizer trim wheel

Above Close up of the turret housing the
Westinghouse AN/AVQ-22 Steerable TV System
(STV), one of the two sensors of the AN/ASQ-
151 Electro-optical Viewing System. The STV
window is heated by means of transparent
electrically conductive film between the glass
laminations to maintain a temperature range
from 86°F to 98°F regardless of the outside
temperature. The STV can view selected areas
within 45° on either side, 15° upward and 45°
downward *(Jim Dunn)*

Top right Details of the inflight refuelling
receptacle with two slipway doors. Switches for
controlling the opening and closing of these
doors are located along with other inflight
refuelling controls in a roof panel within easy
reach of the aircraft commander and copilot
Right The B-52 main gear, seen here from the
rear of the aircraft, is comprised of four twin-
wheel bogies. For landings in crosswind
conditions, the four bogies can be turned up to
20° left or right from centre, thus keeping the
nose of the aircraft into the wind. The maximum
of 20° enable landings to be made in
crosswinds up to 43 knots blowing 90° to the
runway, an important feature as most B-52
bases have only one runway. *(Jim Dunn)*

Top left The single-wheel tip gears retract laterally into the wing, just inboard of the 700-US gallon fixed external tanks. The track, centreline tip gear to tip gear, is 148 feet 5 inches. Prior to the G model, B-52s carried 3000-gallon jettisonable external tanks

Left The normal pneumatic engine starting procedure is sequential and is initiated with the No 4 engine. During alert operations all eight engines are started simultaneously by means of cartridges

Above A maintenance cart has been specially devised to store cowl rings and side panels while engines are serviced. The red and yellow cart is used when oil is drained from the engines

Overleaf The No 3 nacelle, located inboard beneath the right wing, houses the Nos 5 and 6 engines. An engine-driven hydraulic pump, an AC generator, and a constant-speed drive unit can be seen beneath the No 5 engine. Each J57-P-43WB is 'flat rated' to develop 'wet' take-off thrust of 13,750 lb at sea level at temperatures between 20°F and 100°F. Without water injection, the J57-P-43WB has a military rated thrust at sea level of 11,200 lb and a normal rated thrust of 9,500 lb. The B-52G engines are built both by Pratt & Whitney and Ford

31

GS PSI

MHU-83C/E

BUFF weapons

Left Conceived as a strategic bomber carrying free-fall nuclear and thermonuclear bombs, the B-52 was first used as a conventional bomber during the Vietnam War. Today, the BUFF's conventional bombing capability is increasingly emphasized in SAC's planning and, since January 1987, all bomber squadrons are 'dual-docked', meaning that they are trained for both nuclear and conventional missions. Typical of the behind the scenes training activities for conventional operations is the need to learn to load 'iron' bombs as practised here by personnel from the 320th Munitions Maintenance Squadron at Mather AFB. *(Jim Dunn)*

Above In the strategic bombing role, the internal weapons load of the B-52G consists of four B28 thermonuclear bombs in the forward portion of the bomb bay and six AGM-69A SRAMs on a rotary launcher in the aft portion of the bay. Each of the four B28Fls free fall or parachute-retarded laydown stores seen here on a mounting craddle has a yield of up to 1.45 Mt. The warhead of each of the SRAMs has a yield of 200 Kt. Thus, the internal weapon load of a B-52G has the staggering destructive power of nearly 500 bombs such as the *Little Boy* dropped on Hiroshima. *(Karl Kornchuk)*

For use in anti-surface warfare operations as provided in the 1975 USAF-USN Collateral Functions Agreement, B-52Gs have been adapted to carry six AGM-84 Harpoon sea-skimming missiles on each of their wing pylons. The window for the Hughes AN/AAQ-6 Forward Looking Infrared (FLIR) set and Westinghouse AN/AVQ-22 Steerable TV System (STV) are well in evidence

Inset In September 1982, the 320th Bombardment Wing was selected to be the lead unit in a programme to test the compatibility of the B-52G with the Harpoon anti-ship missile. Two crews and an aircraft were dedicated to the demonstration, which culminated with three live launches in 1983. Harpoons were then placed in service with the 42nd BMW at Loring AFB, Maine, and the 43rd BMW at Andersen AFB, Guam. More recently, other B-52G wings have begun training for Harpoon operations. These five AGM-84As were carried by a B-52G of the 320th photographed at Mather AFB on 12 November 1987

Left Taken at March AFB on 15 May 1965, this photograph of 53-0372, the last of the 27 RB-52Bs built in Seattle, shows the twin 20 mm cannon and A-3A fire control system fitted to early production aircraft. The tail gunner's lot was a lonely one as the only connection between the turret and the forward pressurized compartment housing the rest of the crew was a narrow crawlway. However, prior to using the crawlway it was necessary to depressurize the cabin and hence the gunner tended to stay alone for the duration of the flight

Above The MD-9 fire control system and four 0.50-in machine guns of B-52Ds proved surprisingly effective against MiGs during *Linebacker II*, the 11-day offensive against North Vietnam in December 1972 and January 1973. Two victories were confirmed and three more counted as probables. This quartet of 'fifties' in the tail of 56-0676 got the first enemy fighter to be shot down by a B-52 gunner, a MiG-21 brought down near Hanoi during the night of 18 December 1972

Above Starting with the B-52G, the gunner was moved from the tail turret to the main compartment where he occupies a rearward-facing seat on the right of the Electronic Warfare Officer (EWO). The B-52Gs guns are still 0.50-in M3s but are now slaved to the AN/ASG-15 fire control system. The radome immediately above the gun houses ECM antennas for the AN/APR-25 and AN/ALQ-117, that above housing the search radar for the AN/ASG-15. The small white radome above the aft fuselage is for

another AN/ALQ-117 antenna and the side fairing covers a cooling exhaust for some of the ECM equipment

Right Photographed at Edwards AFB on 8 November 1987, this B-52G tail turret is of the standard configuration. However, the test device on the lower right gun is unidentified. Standard ammunition load for each M3 machine gun is 600 rounds

Rear defence for the B-52H is provided by a six-barrel 20 mm T171 cannon and its associated AN/ASG-21 fire control system. Hot shot F-15 jockeys are often brutally reminded not to be too complacent during Red Flag exercises when they suddenly find themselves being tracked by B-52 gunners as they try to intercept BUFFs flying in and out of canyons

BUFF markings

Left Before being camouflaged, B-52s were adorned with large emblems painted over a star-studded blue band on the nose. The SAC shield was on the left side and the wing's insignia on the right. Representative wing's emblems are shown in this series of B-52 nose details:

70th BMW, Clinton-Sherman AFB, OK: B-52E-95-BO (57-0029)

22nd BMW, March AFB, CA: B-52E-90-BO (57-0020)

96th BMW, Dyess AFB, TX: B-57E-60-BW (57-0113)

93rd BOMBARDMENT WING

0159

3rd BMW, Castle AFB, CA: B-52F-70-BW (57-0159)

319th BMW, Grand Forks, ND: B-52H-145-BW (60-0035)

340th BMW, Bergstrom AFB, TX: B-52B-35-BO (53-0397)

410th BMW, K I Sawyer, MI: B-52H-145-BW (60-0031)

449th BMW, Kincheloe AFB, MI: B-52H-155-BW (60-0049)

450th BMW, Minot AFB, ND: B-52H-160-BW (60-0050)

494th BMW, Sheppard AFB, TX: B-52B-35-BO (53-0392)

Left The use of tail markings on B-52s was not officially approved until 1987. However, temporary tail markings were applied on a number of special occasions, such as when units participated in bombing competitions. This attractive winged 2 was applied on B-52Fs when the 2nd Bombardment Wing participated in the Royal Air Force Strike Command's Bombing and Navigation Competition from 17 to 24 April 1971

Current unit tail markings are often quite discrete as shown by those applied to B-52Gs of the 2nd BMW at Barksdale AFB, Lousiana. A black fleur-de-lys is painted on the fin, below the radio call number and above the fairings for the AN/ALQ-153. *Barksdale* is painted in grey old English script on the outboard of the external tanks. *(Brian C Rogers)*

Above The winged death's head now painted on the fin of B-52Hs of the Bombardment Wing goes back to the insignia approved for the 5th Group (Composite) on 21 June 1924. The forebear of the 5th BMW was then based at Luke Field, Territory of Hawaii

Right A black moose's head, with blue eyes and nostrils and a blue bomb in his mouth, now identifies B-52Gs from the 42nd Bombardment Wing based at Loring AFB, Maine. This wing converted from Convair B-36s to B-52Cs in 1956, exchanged its early Stratofortresses for B-52Ds in 1957, and has flown B-52Gs since 1959. *(Brian C Rogers)*

Top right As befits a Texas-based unit, the 7th BMW from Carswell AFB, seven miles from downtown Fort Worth, has incorporated a rendering of a Texas longhorn in its tail markings. For those of us who were not too good in geography to learn where Fort Worth is or who have not seen enough western movies to recognize a longhorn, the 7th BMW has kindly added the name of its home state. Thanks to the maintenance crew of 60-0053 who added 'zaps' on the left external tank, our geography lesson continues: the yellow and black 'atoll' is for a deployment to Diego Garcia, the red 'hang loose' for a stopover in Hawaii. *(Brian C Rogers)*

While still qualifying as a subdued marking, the sea eagle of the 92nd Bombardment Wing at Fairchild AFB, Washington, is original both in terms of graphic and colours. 61-0040, a B-52H-170-BW, is the 744th and last Stratofortress. It was accepted by the Air Force on 26 October 1962

Right Located between Merced and Atwater in central California and named after Brigadier General Frederick W Castle, Castle AFB has adopted a logical tail marking for the B-52Gs of its 93rd Bombardment Wing: a castle tower

Overleaf The flaming arrow insignia applied to the tail of B-52Gs from the 97th Bombardment Wing at Blythville AFB, Arkansas, is quite appropriate. Firstly, it has been part of the insignia of the 97th since March 1943 when the emblem of its forebear, the 97th Bombardment Group, was approved. Secondly, it recalls skirmishes fought against Indians in the then Arkansas Territory. *(97th BMW/PA)*

Above Sticking out of a maintenance hangar at Mather AFB, the tail of 59-2593 displays the markings applied in 1987 to aircraft of the 320th Bombardment Wing. The bear, which is part of the California flag, and sunburst were fitting for a unit based outside of Sacramento, the state capital

Right Triangle K tail markings were first applied to B-17s of the 379th Bombardment Group when that unit began combat operations from Kimbolton in 1943. They were briefly resurrected in 1980 for the SAC Bombing Competition and are now adorning B-52Gs of the 379th BMW at Wurtsmith AFB, Michigan. *(379th BMW/PA)*

Top right The more recent tail markings of the 320th BMW, first applied to 57-6497 in January 1988, combine a larger California bear with the base name but no longer feature a sunburst. Noteworthy is the fact that since the inactivation of its 904th AREFS in October 1986, the 320th BMW is the only Air Force wing with a single flying squadron, the 441st Bombardment Squadron

The un-cryptic tail markings worn by the BUFFs of the 43rd Bombardment Wing at Andersen AFB, Guam, during the Vietnam War. *(43rd BMW/PA)*

Based at Griffiss AFB in upstate New York, the
668th Bombardment Squadron, 416th
Bombardment Wing, has quite appropriately
selected the Statue of Liberty to adorn the tail of
its B-52Gs. *(Bud Joyce)*

In the past SAC has frowned on the use of nose art on B-52s. Hence, 58-0210, a B-52G-100-BW of the 93rd Bombardment Wing, carried this bold Bald Eagle marking only briefly in August 1984. Fortunately for aviation enthusiasts, General John T Chain, Jr, the current CINCSAC (SAC's Commander in Chief), was recently quoted as being in favour of nose art on aircraft. *(Tony Muniz)*

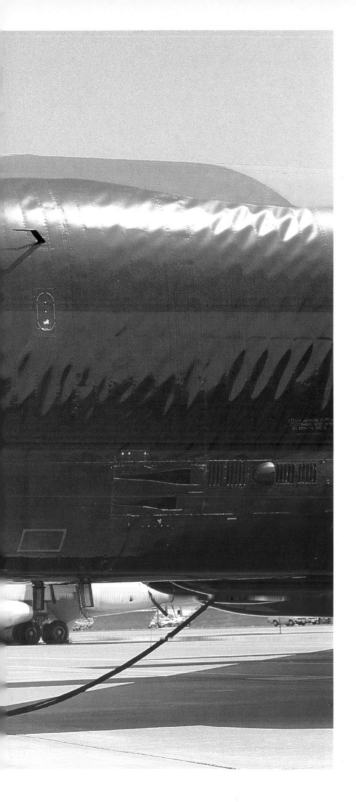

BUFFs
in warpaint

Long after the Southeast Asia War had ended and anti-war feelings had given place to revived national pride, 'MiG-killers' began sprouting red stars nearly rivalling in size their US national markings. This was not only the case with fighters but also with at least one B-52D. On 18 December 1972, during the first *Linebacker II* mission, SSgt Samuel O Turner, the gunner of 56-0676, shot down a MiG-21. More than eight years later, this B-52D was adorned conspicuously with a kill marking on both sides of its forward fuselage

Above 'The MiG-killer' B-52D of the 22nd Bombardment Wing landing at Beale AFB on 30 May 1980. Subsequently transferred to the 43rd Strategic Wing at Andersen AFB, 56-0676 became the last active B-52D before being retired on 1 October 1983. Late during the Southeast Asia War, the B-52Ds which had been retrofitted with the 'big belly' bomb bay for conventional operations received a new camouflage with extended black under surfaces and black vertical tail surfaces

Top right Taxying at Castle AFB on 19 April 1979, this camouflaged B-52H from the last production block appears to be sailing in a sea of yellow grasses. It would not have taken much of a spark to get a good grass fire going, thus probably prompting the airfield manager to send a cleaning crew on a weed abatement party to prevent a potential disaster

Right Landing at Castle AFB on 8 June 1971, this B-52F of the 93rd Bombardment Wing shows well the different schemes used on engine nacelles and external tanks

72

These pages and overleaf The oddest camouflage scheme seen on BUFFs was that applied in 1968 to some B-52Hs of the 449th and 450th Bombardment Wings, Belonging to the 449th BMW, 60-0013 was photographed at Kincheloe AFB on 10 July 1968, while 60-0066 and 61-0037, both assigned to the 450th BMW, were photographed six days later at Minot AFB. If nothing else, this scheme did put much in evidence the distinctive shape of the nacelles housing the TF33 turbofans powering the H model

Approaching McClelland AFB on 1 December 1971, and believed to be an aircraft from the 4200th Test Wing—a mysterious unit which was based at Beale AFB in the late sixties and early seventies and reportedly had B-52Gs modified to carry and launch Lockheed D-21 supersonic reconnaissance drones—59-2596 shows that it has been fitted with an unusual pylon between its Nos 1 and 2 nacelles

BUFF people

Left Not lifting his eyes from his work, Airman First Class Christopher A Beasley appears to be telling the photographer where to go. Actually, he is directing the fork lift operator to move right to pick up a Mk 82 for loading aboard a B-52G

With the aid of his check list, Sgt Christopher Hubbard, a weapons loader from the 320th BMW, verifies that a Mk 82 'iron' bomb has been safely loaded in the rear of a B-52G bomb bay

To assure the success of a long training sortie, the next most important item after carefully following safety procedures is to have enough coffee on board! Captain Andre M Provoncha, a radar navigator with the 441st Bombardment Squadron, loads the precious cargo

While Captain Provoncha is in charge of coffee, his fellow navigator, Captain Robert S Huml, loads cases and other personal paraphernalia prior to joining the other crew members in preflighting 59-2565 before their departure for a morning sortie on 12 November 1987

Oh, those darned flyboys! Why do they have to run up their eight engines just as my favourite song is being played. Airman First Class William Markham, a security policeman at Mather AFB, tries to keep in touch with Base Security as the engines of a nearby B-52G of the 320th BMW are being run up. The KC-135E in the background belongs to the co-located 314th AREFS, 940th AREFG, one of three AFRES squadrons flying Stratotankers

Overleaf, left Major Ed Rice, a pilot with the 441st Bombardment Squadron, 320th Bombardment Wing, in the bomb bay of 59-2565 during preflight inspection on 12 November 1987. Above his head can be seen the narrow crawlway providing access between the pressurized forward compartment and the aft equipment compartment beneath the fin

Overleaf, right Sergeant Charles W Stevenson, a bombing navigation flightline specialist with the 320th BMW, takes good care of the window covering the Westinghouse AN/AVQ-22 Steerable TV System. The STV has greatly improved the BUFF's ability to penetrate enemy defences by flying in weather at less than 200 ft altitude

83

Top left Oh, these early morning flights! Captain Robert S Huml, radar navigator, steps out of the crew bus to begin preflighting the aircraft. By then, he and his fellow crew members have already been up for at least a couple of hours, checking weather and going through the final briefing steps

Right Lieutenant Colonel Neal D Coyle, the 441st BMS Squadron Commander, during his preflight walk-around on 12 November 1987. The previous day, while flying 57-6468, the oldest B-52G in the inventory, Colonel Coyle and his crew ran into a bald eagle during a low-level training sortie above the Montana-Wyoming border. The eagle lost. But not before ripping out the nose radome and punching a hole in the forward bulkhead, forcing the crew to abort the mission and return to Mather AFB. *(Jim Dunn)*

Left Leaving nothing to chance, the aircraft commander carefully inspects the forward right bogie of the main undercarriage. One of the two landing lights, incorporated in the forward gear door on each side, can be seen. In addition to these landing lights, B-52Gs are equipped with a crosswind landing light on the right forward landing gear (not visible from this angle) and three taxi lights (one in the leading edge of each wing just outboard of the outboard nacelles and one coupled with the crosswind landing light). *(Jim Dunn)*

Top left Airman First Class Lukenbill, a flight line engine specialist, closes the cowling after completing his inspection of the No 3 engine of a B-52G of the 320th Bombardment Wing

Left Sergeant Smith, of the 320th Organizational Maintenance Squadron, proudly wears his 1987 SAC Bomb-Nav Competition patch. A 320th BMW crew won the conventional bombing competition while a 940th AREFS crew, the Reserve tanker squadron sharing the Mather ramp with the 320th BMW, teamed up with other AFRES KC-135 crews to win this year's Saunders Trophy

Top right Like many of today's BUFF crew members, 2Lt Rick Bell was 'knee high to a grasshopper' when B-52s were already dropping bombs in Vietnam. Fresh from Undergraduate Pilot Training (UPT), Rick is carefully making notes on his ONC chart in preparation for the next day's training sortie during which his skills as a copilot will be evaluated by instructors from the 328th Bombardment Squadron

Bottom right While a veteran instructor of the 93rd BMW closes his eyes in concentration, a young navigator, just graduated from the navigator course at Mather AFB as evidenced by his 87-10 class patch on his left shoulder, carefully follows briefing steps on his tech manual

Top left Typically, crew members fly B-52s for six to nine years prior to being given staff positions for 'career broadening'. After 'flying a desk' for three to four years, they must again go to Castle AFB for refresher training prior to joining their new unit. Lieutenant Colonel Evans, seen here in the aircraft commander's seat of a B-52G of the 328th Bombardment Squadron, the B-52 flying training squadron, already wears the patch of the squadron to which he has been assigned, the 325th BMS flying B-52Hs from Fairchild AFB

Left Low-level flying can be rough for the radar-navigator and navigator confined on the lower deck where their only view of the outside world is provided by the EVS monitors

Above Major Tom Rayl, an instructor with the 328th Bombardment Squadron at Castle AFB, patiently stares in the depth of the STV turret for the benefit of the photographer

Left With microphone and headset plugged into a B-52G external microphone system, a ground crewman of the 320th BMW, stands by for starting engines

Overleaf The back wall of the crew lounge in the 328th Bombardment Squadron's building at Mather AFB has recently been redecorated by a talented squadron member. The painting is right up to date as shown by the pair of Sukhoi Su-27 *Flanker B* fighters on the left side

Used to carry flight helmet, headset, gloves, check list, and other small items, flight bags come in handy. Patches on one of the three bags about to be taken aboard a B-52G at Castle AFB are that of the 1981 SAC Bomb-Nav Competition and that of the 524th Bombardment Squadron, the B-52G squadron of the 379th Bombardment Wing at Wurtsmith AFB, Michigan. This unit won the General John D Ryan B-52 Trophy by obtaining the most points in the low-level bombing phase of the 1987 Proud Shield SAC Bomb-Nav Competition

Young BUFFs

After taking advantage of a bright winter afternoon doing touch-and-go landings for two hours, 57-6495 comes to the end of its full landing with drag chute billowing in the late afternoon sun. The crew appears to have had a fuel transfer problem as the right tip gear is firmly on the runway and the left wing is up

Above The white fairing above the forward fuselage of this B-52H-165-BW of the 5th Bombardment Wing covers the receive/transmit antenna of the AN/ASC-19 AFSATCOM (Air Force SATellite COMunications system). This relatively recent modification permits secure teletype satellite communication on UHF frequencies

Top right 58-0178, a B-52G-95-BW of the 328th Bombardment Squadron/93rd Bombardment Wing, on the ramp at Castle AFB on 5 August 1986. Temperature in the welcome shade provided by the right wing and No 3 nacelle of another B-52Gs was 104°F, a not unusual summer occurrence in the San Joaquin Valley

Right Showing that he has not lost his touch after 'flying a desk' for several years, Lt Col Evans deftly and steadily holds TUFT 88 in position behind and below TEASE 34 while both fly along the refuelling track located east of Lassen Volcanic National Park in northern California

Gear up and flaps down, B-52G 57-6495 goes
around for its umpteenth touch-and-go of the
day. The late afternoon winter light clearly sets
out the 'farms' of ECM blade antennas beneath
the fuselage, fore and aft of the wings, and the
data link antenna atop the rear fuselage

Above No, no, no, Alfred! I've told you a hundred times that you must position yourself below and behind the tanker . . . A B-52G and a KC-135R appear to have it all wrong as they fly by during an open house show at Castle AFB on 28 June 1987. In addition to training all B-52 crews, the 93rd Bombardment Wing has two KC-135 squadrons. The 93rd AREFS, which trains all 135 flight crews, and the 924th AREFS, which is an operational squadron, share a large number of KC-135As as well as a few re-engined KC-135Rs

Top right Photographed at Homestead AFB, 58-0231 shows off the attractive markings now applied to the tail and external tanks of B-52Gs from the 668th Bombardment Squadron, 416th Bombardment Wing. Based at Griffiths AFB, New York, the 416th BMW became in January 1981 the first SAC wing to receive ALCMs (Air Launched Cruise Missiles). Nine months later, it attained operational status with the new missile. *(Bud Joyce)*

Right Framed by two KC-135As of the 93rd Bombardment Wing, this B-52G-95-BW (58-0164) taxies past the control tower at Castle AFB at the start of a training sortie in the afternoon of 4 August 1986

The 7th Bombardment Wing made the front page of newspapers in November 1986 when it put into service the 132nd Stratofortress modified to carry AGM-86B cruise missiles. Delivery of this aircraft placed the United States in breach of the 1979 Strategic Arms Limitation Treaty (the so-called SALT 2 agreement). With AGM-86Bs on its starboard pylon and an MHU-173/E ALCM loading trailer parked next to it, this B-52H of the 7th BMW was photographed at Carswell AFB more than thirteen months earlier when most people were unaware that the wing already had cruise missiles. *(Brian C Rogers)*

Overleaf Trying to break through low lying morning fog, the sun casts a pale glow over the ramp at Mather AFB as a B-52G of the 320th BMW is being readied on 12 November 1987. Three months later, SAC announced that this wing would soon relinquish its nuclear deterrence role and that henceforth its B-52Gs would only carry conventional weapons, including gravity bombs, precision munitions, Harpoons and mines

It rains even in California (unfortunately not often enough during the past two years). On the morning of 17 November 1987, however, the broad wing of the B-52 was a welcome shelter from which to photograph the work of the maintenance crews while hoping that the weather would clear before our late morning takeoff

Overleaf Although assigned to the 328th Bombardment Squadron, a unit which is primarily providing inflight training for B 52 crews, 58-0244 is one of the 92 B-52Gs which have been modified to carry cruise missiles as indicated by the distinctive wing root fairing added to cruise-missile carrying aircraft. As stipulated in the 1979 Strategic Arms Limitation Treaty, B-52Gs and Hs modified to carry cruise missiles have been fitted with wing root extensions to enable the Soviets to verify by means of satellite photography that the number of aircraft so modified remains as provided by the SALT agreement

60-0060, a B-52H-165-BW of the 23rd Bombardment Squadron, 5th Bombardment Wing, photographed from the control tower at Travis AFB. The 5th BMW was based at Travis between February 1959 and July 1968 but Minot AFB has been its home for the past 20 years

Above Due to its undercarriage configuration, the Stratofortress lands in a flat attitude as demonstrated by this B-52G-120-BW about to settle on the runway at Mather AFB on a grey November morning

Top right 61-0018, a B-52H-170-BW of the 644th Bombardment Squadron, 410th Bombardment wing, during a stopover at Carswell AFB on 3 February 1987

Right With stormy tropical skies as a background, 59-2594, a B-52G-120-BW of the 2nd BMW, makes a final turn to line up with the runway at Tyndall AFB, Florida, on 22 September 1978, at the end of a sortie during which it served as a target for interceptors taking part in the William Tell '78 meet. The 2nd and 7th Bombardment Wing are unique among current wings in having two B-52 squadrons, those at Barksdale AFB being the 62nd and 596th, and those at Carswell being the 9th and 20th

Right By the fall of 1982, only three wings—the 7th at Carswell AFB, the 22nd at March AFB, and the 43rd at Andersen AFB (where 56-0617 was photographed on 22 October 1982)—were still equipped with B-52Ds. The last operational B-52D was retired by the 43rd Strategic Wing on 1 October 1983 but the final B-52D ferry flights were made by the 7th BMW. On 4 October 1983, 55-0674 was the last flown to Davis-Monthan AFB to be placed in storage at MASDC. On 20 February 1984, 56-0687 became the last to fly when it was ferried from Carswell to Florida to be placed on permanent display at the Orlando International Airport

Left This B-52H-160-BW (60-0051) of the 7th Bombardment Wing at Carswell AFB on 11 October 1986 is fitted with external racks for carrying 'iron' bombs. When in 1964 B-52s were modified to carry conventional bombs externally, the pylon normally used to carry AGM-28 Hound Dog missiles were fitted with beams to which were attached MERs (Multiple Ejection Racks). This temporary 'mod' soon became a permanent fixture and is still used by B-52Gs and Hs. *(Brian C Rogers)*

Left With MSgt Sam Hunt operating the boom, 58-0190 takes on fuel while flying along the eastern slopes of the Sierra Nevada before proceeding to Tinker AFB, Oklahoma, where it was to undergo overhaul at the Oklahoma City Air Logistics Center

See and be seen. With landing and taxi lights switched on as a safety precaution, 57-6484 comes in to land at Castle AFB on 23 May 1984

Overleaf Dark and looking ominous, 60-0053 skims over the clouds above New Mexico during a training sortie on 2 April 1987. Not yet modified to carry AGM-86 cruise missiles, this B-52H-160-BW of the 7th Bombardment Wing has the standard wing root fairing. *(Brian C Rogers)*

Above Ever since the 1940s, most SAC bases have been located in northern tier states where winters are long and cold. Fortunately, B-52s, such as these aircraft of the 92nd BMW at Loring AFB in February 1987, take well to snow and ice operations. Some of their crews, particularly those in maintenance who have to work outside in the bitter cold, find it more difficult to adapt to this harsh environment. *(Karl Kornchuk)*

Top right During the winter months, as soon as morning fog has dispersed, Castle AFB becomes a beehive of activities with B-52Gs and KC-135As and Rs departing on long training missions while others remain close to base as crews practice emergencies and touch-and-goes. Each year approximately 100 bomber crews and 200 tanker crews are trained by the 93rd Bombardment Wing

Right B-52G-110-BW (58-0238) on take-off at Castle AFB, California, on 18 November 1987. The dense black smoke evidences the use of water injection to increase maximum thrust to 13,750 lb per engine. The 1200 US gallon water supply tank is located in the fuselage aft of the crew compartment

Unlike earlier Stratofortress versions which had both ailerons and spoilers, the B-52Gs and B-52Hs only have spoilers. Each wing is provided with seven spoilers, as seen on the right wing of 58-0190, which are used for lateral control and, when deployed simultaneously on both wings, as airbrakes

Overleaf During the late forties the runways at Fairfield-Suisun AFB, California, were extended and widened to accommodate Convair B-36s. Although control of this base, which had been renamed Travis AFB in 1951, was transferred to the Military Air Transport Service in 1955, it remained the home of the 5th BMW until 1968. Now housing the C-5s and C-141s of the 60th Military Airlift Wing, Travis AFB is frequently used by the 93rd BMW to familiarize new B-52 'drivers' with operations away from Castle AFB. (Carl E Porter)

To have the same total take-off thrust as the turbofan-powered B-52H, the B-52G would have had to be fitted with an extra pair of J57 turbojets. Moreover, as demonstrated by this B-52H of the 5th Bombardment Wing taking off from Travis AFB on 29 June 1987, the TF33-P-3 turbofan generates 17,000 lb of thrust without recourse to water injection and thus B-52Hs are not trailed by dense clouds of smoke when they get airborne